TAKE OFF THE BUBBLE WRAP

TAKE OFF THE BUBBLE WRAP

BEYOND PROTECTION: RAISING INDEPENDENT,
RESILIENT AND HAPPY KIDS

SHERRON VALERIOTE

IGUANA

Publisher: Cheryl Hawley
Editor: Amanda Feeney
Front cover design: Linsey Reimer

ISBN 978-1-77180-729-6 (paperback)
ISBN 978-1-77180-728-9 (epub)

This is an original print edition of *Take Off the Bubble Wrap*.

TABLE OF CONTENTS

PROLOGUE

Research shows that children growing up under constant protection aren't well prepared for the real world, while those exposed to challenges develop the toughness needed to thrive in any environment.

Imagine a seed planted in a greenhouse, nurtured in ideal conditions. It's watered on a strict schedule, fertilized just right, and protected by controlled temperatures, humidity, and light. Under these perfect conditions, the seed grows into a flawless, vibrant flower, every petal pristine and delicate. If you take that greenhouse flower and transplant it outside, it struggles, its delicate structure ill-equipped for the rough conditions.

Now consider the same seed planted outdoors, where it must weather the unpredictability of the natural world. It faces gusting winds, heavy rains, periods of drought, scorching heat, and chilling cold. Though it may lack the greenhouse flower's flawless appearance, it grows stronger, adapting to its surroundings and developing the resilience needed to endure hardships.

Like these flowers, children who grow up in a protective bubble are not prepared for the slings and arrows of the real world. But children who learn to adapt to the world around them develop the resilience they need to blossom.

INTRODUCTION

THE IMPORTANCE OF

RESILIENCE

*Success depends upon previous preparation,
and without such preparation, there is sure to
be failure.*

— Confucius

As parents, our hearts naturally ache to protect our children from every bump, bruise, and disappointment. We want to shield them from the struggles we experienced, smooth their paths, and guide them toward happy, successful lives. While it's natural to want to protect our kids, the way we go about it can make all the difference. Sometimes our well-meaning efforts to shelter them end up wrapping them in a bubble — keeping them safe but also holding them back from growing into emotionally strong, independent adults.

In modern parenting, the desire to shield children from failure and discomfort has led to a phenomenon known as over-parenting (or helicopter parenting or snowplow parenting). This well-intentioned but misguided parenting approach often results in children who are ill-prepared for the realities of life. By constantly swooping in to solve problems, parents inadvertently prevent their children from developing crucial problem-solving and emotional-regulation skills. As a result, these children grow up with a diminished ability to cope with stress, failure, and adversity.

Consider the following story about over-parenting:

Before Karen takes her five-year-old son, Foster, to his first soccer practice, she covers all his exposed skin with SPF 75 sunscreen and makes sure he wears his new sun hat. In her bag, she packs extra socks, a Ziploc bag of fresh orange slices, a water bottle, a first aid kit, and a laminated

list of emergency numbers. She intently watches Foster play, and when he trips and falls over his new soccer shoes, she rushes onto the field, scoops him up, and carries him away.

Karen has the best intentions. She wants to protect her son from serious harm. She imagines broken bones, sunstroke, dehydration, and maybe an emergency room visit. The chance that any of these things happen during the ten minutes that Foster is playing are slim. The unfortunate drawback of this type of over-parenting is that the child, while watching and listening to his parent, is sensing that playing soccer is risky behaviour. Karen may unintentionally pass a fear of risk or a fear of trying new things on to her child.

Our children are growing up in an era of unprecedented technological advancement, social complexity, and global interconnectedness. They're exposed to news of famine, climate change, sexual assault, political unrest, wildfires, floods, and mass shootings. They face relentless pressures: high academic expectations, drugs, bullying, family breakdown, the search for sexual identity, and also almost-impossible-to-avoid social media. The modern child navigates a landscape far more intricate than that of any previous generation.

It is in this context that the principles of resilience become not just beneficial but essential. In today's fast-paced, ever-changing world, raising resilient children has never been more crucial. As parents, educators, and caregivers, we are tasked with the monumental responsibility of preparing the next generation for the complexities of adulthood. Yet, in our quest to provide the best for our children, we often find ourselves in a paradox:

Our efforts to protect and nurture sometimes inadvertently lead to the very fragility we seek to avoid.

By encouraging resilience in our young children, we're preparing them for a life on their own when they leave the shelter of our parental embrace. Some young people today find starting life on their own difficult. Depression and anxiety in college-age students has doubled since 2004. According to Jonathan Haidt, author of *The Anxious Generation,* one underlying cause seems to be that we've raised a generation of emotionally fragile children.

Young adults who have no experience making their own decisions, taking responsibility, and living with the consequences of their decision — and who have not faced disappointments or failures — are not ready to set out on their own. They become easily overwhelmed by the realities facing them in the world outside the protection of their family, which contributes to anxiety and depression in young adulthood. As Greg Lukianoff and Jonathan Haidt point out in their book, *The Coddling of the American Mind,* "the resulting culture of safetyism … interferes with young people's social, emotional, and intellectual development. It makes it harder for them to become autonomous adults who are able to navigate the bumpy road of life." Resilience and independence are the foundations of a successful life.

The goal of this book is to provide a roadmap to help parents encourage their children to develop this necessary resilience and independence. Parenting has no rules or guidelines. Parents are already overloaded with information, advice, and directions about the best ways to raise children in the current climate. Grandparents,

parents, in-laws, friends — and, of course, social media already deliver countless ideas, philosophies, critiques, and expectations on how to raise children.

Many parents today feel overwhelmed with trying to be the "perfect" parent and raise "perfect" children. But there's no such thing as a perfect parent or a perfect child. Most new parents start their parenting journey with a box full of their own experiences, past hurts, prejudices, religious beliefs, successes, educational experiences, political views, financial situations, sexual identities, and so on. And they often start with predetermined views on child-raising.

Parenting is difficult. It's no wonder that many young parents are feeling anxious and often wonder if they're good enough. They may ask themselves: Am I doing the right thing? Am I too lenient? Am I too strict? Is my child in the right school? Are they being stimulated enough? Should my child have more friends? Is my child getting the marks needed to get into the right high school or college? Should they participate in more or fewer after-school activities? Should I limit screen time? At the heart of all these questions is the desire to see their child be successful and happy. And the best way to do that is to help them develop the skills they need to solve their own problems, bounce back from setbacks, and create their own path forward.

Our role as parents should not be to remove obstacles from our children's path but to prepare them to navigate those obstacles with confidence and competence. We must teach them to understand and manage their emotions, encourage them to take healthy risks, and allow them to experience and learn from failure.

Preparing our children for life's inevitable challenges requires more than just shielding them from harm; it demands that we equip them with the tools, mindset, and character to face and overcome those challenges.

So how do we raise children resilient enough to not only face the future but also to thrive in it? Fostering resilience begins when your child is very young. In this book, I focus on children under the age of eleven — toddlers and grade-school-aged children. I draw upon my professional experience as a licensed couple and family therapist and my personal experience as a mother and grandmother to suggest how a parent might foster resilience in their child. I also include what I've learned from interviews with parents of young children, grandparents, and current professionals in the fields of education, mental health, and child protection.

You'll find practical tips to help you teach your children how to face challenges and to prepare them for a future in which they can thrive. We'll explore the key elements that contribute to resilience, from fostering emotional intelligence to embracing failure as a learning tool and encouraging independent behaviour. Each chapter is designed to offer practical advice backed by current research and real-life examples. At the end of each chapter, you'll find questions to help you reflect on how you are fostering resilience in your children.

As we delve into the strategies and principles that underpin resilience, it's important to recognize that each child is unique. Many children must also adapt to life with limitations and disabilities. There's no one-size-fits-all approach to parenting. The insights and recommendations in this book should be adapted to fit the needs and personality of your child. Resilience is not a destination but a journey, one that requires patience, empathy, and a willingness to let go of perfection.

Ultimately, the goal of this book is to empower you as a parent, educator, or caregiver and to provide you with the tools you need to foster resilience. You'll learn how to let go of some of the worries and how to trust in your child's ability to navigate life. And you'll prepare them to not only survive but also to thrive in the face of life's challenges. By fostering resilience in your children, you are giving them the gift of strength, adaptability, and confidence.

Reflection Questions

What kind of a world will my child be living in when they grow up?

How is my child's world different from mine when I was their age?

CHAPTER 1

WHAT DOES

RESILIENCE MEAN?

You're stronger than you think, braver than you feel and smarter than you know.

— A.A. Milne

Resilience can be defined in many ways. To some, it means having self-confidence. To others, it means having the ability to adapt, recover, and thrive when faced with challenges. It can also mean being self-sufficient, having grit, or being strong, tough, durable, and flexible. In this book I define resilience as all of the above. We live in a world where participation trophies are handed out to everyone, where no one fails a test, where there are no winners or losers. This may lead to the conclusion that young children don't need to be resilient to function well in their world. Instead we may think that outstanding political figures or super athletes or war heroes are resilient. But everyone needs resilience — to get up every day and go to work, to stay up all night with an ill child, to study hard for an exam, to cope with the loss of a parent, or to handle a bad review at work.

So why do children need to be resilient? Children live with and depend on their parents for the first twenty or so years of their lives. But after that, they'll live most of their lives without their parents, and so we need to prepare them to survive and thrive when they venture out into the world on their own. Our challenge as parents is to find ourselves out of a parenting job by the time our children are eighteen to twenty years old. Your child should be able to function without you as they merge into the adult world. That doesn't mean you won't continue to support, love, and guide your adult child at this stage of their life. You can continue to do those things throughout their adult lives. But by the time your child becomes a young adult, most of the basic teaching, nurturing, guiding, and supporting that you've done during their youth will be over, and you'll hope they can function well in the real world without you.

To accomplish this, we need to teach children who are still in their formative years to face the challenges of their current life. As they grow and develop, we need to help them navigate some common age-appropriate challenges, such as school stress, friendships, and family changes. We can start this when they're very young by establishing routines, helping them learn to control and express emotions appropriately, and exposing them to the social norms of their family and their community. These steps will help lay the foundation a child needs to navigate their world without excessive stress.

Routine

Most children function better when their day is predictable. Establishing a morning routine for your child, whether they are six months or six years old, helps them start their day with less chaos and more predictability. Your child will learn from an early age that preparing for the day ahead reduces anxiety. Age-appropriate routines can include simple tasks, like brushing their teeth, combing their hair, making their bed, and eating a good breakfast.

Explaining your plans for the day will also provide your child with a feeling of security — even if the plans change as the day goes on. This can be as simple as saying, "Today you'll go to school, and after the bus drops you off at home in the afternoon, you'll have a snack, and then I'll take you to soccer practice" or "Today you'll go to school, and after school I'll pick you up and take you to the dentist. So for today, you'll have to miss playing with your friends after school."

Establishing a bedtime routine is also helpful. Parents often find that it gives their child a chance to have some quiet time and to settle before they go to sleep. A bedtime routine might be as simple as reading your child a story, letting your child read on their own, or talking to your child about their day. Older children may include preparing their backpack or choosing an outfit for the next day. Screen time is discouraged at bedtime. Many parents and professionals agree that children under eleven years should not have phones in their bedroom at all.

Controlling and expressing emotions

Knowing how to express emotions is important at all ages. And it's especially important for children. A baby cries to let you know they're hungry or cold or want to be held. Older children may also express how they feel by crying, though their tears may be their way of showing anger, disappointment, or sadness. These expressions of emotion are critical to a child's wellbeing. However, it's equally important for children to learn that they should not let these expressions of emotion overwhelm them.

Parents shouldn't dismiss their children's feelings, and they should help their children find a resolution to their upset. Your child may express their upset by withdrawing, crying, yelling, or screaming. Allowing any of these to go on indefinitely doesn't help your child. Once they've started to calm down, say things like "Tell me what's wrong," "I can see why you might feel that way," and "Let's talk about what we can do about this." Teach your child to move past their upset or disappointment or anger and think about ways to deal with what's bothering them.

Being able to express and control emotions is a critical part of becoming a mature, resilient adult. If children don't practice this when they're young, they may grow into adults who are paralyzed and overwhelmed by their feelings, leaving them unable to move forward or solve problems because their thinking becomes derailed by their emotions.

Family and community social norms

Learning the family's social norms helps your child feel like they belong to the family. It also makes their (and your) experiences within the family go more smoothly. A family's social norms might be eating dinner together every night, going to church every week, comforting others when they are upset, shopping together for school clothes, or watching a particular TV show as a family. Parents may also insist on behaviour-regulating norms, such as not talking with a mouth full of food, washing hands before eating dinner, keeping music at a reasonable volume so that it doesn't interfere with the comfort of others, or taking some time to talk to Grandma when she visits.

Fitting in with the community's social norms helps children feel connected and like they're part of something bigger than their family. It also makes it easier for them to function outside of their home. Community social norms include such things as attending school regularly, obeying traffic rules, and being polite to others.

Children will sometimes reject their family or community social norms in an effort to find their way to an adult life that is different than the one in which they grew up. For some, this can be a painful process, and for others, it can be freeing. In either case, it's essential to support your child's choices as long as they aren't hurting themselves or others.

Learning how to be resilient is an important part of a young child's development. Having routines, learning to regulate and express emotions, and being exposed to social norms can help children navigate the common challenges they face, like school, friendships, and family interactions. It also helps them to develop a healthy pattern of dealing with life, which they will carry into adulthood.

Reflection Questions

What routines do we have in our house?

Who in my life demonstrates resilience?

CHAPTER 2

FEAR OF FAILURE

Start where you are. Use what you have. Do what you can.

— Arthur Ashe

Sometimes children are afraid to try new things because they worry about failing. They're afraid their peers might make fun of them or they'll disappoint their parents. Sometimes they have very high expectations of themselves that they worry they won't live up to. A child's fear can hinder them from having fun, learning new things, or facing challenges with confidence. If this fear lingers, it can impact their adult life as well.

Younger children may view failure simply. But older children and adolescents begin to internalize this fear and may associate failure with a loss of ability or worth.

As adults, they may continue to question themselves or shy away from trying new things, thereby missing opportunities to grow and fulfill their potential.

As parents, it's essential to guide your child beyond this fear so they can grow to be more resilient. Parents can help their children overcome their fear of failure by focusing on effort instead of results, making the home a safe place for making mistakes, encouraging exploration, modelling how to face fear, offering help without taking over, and celebrating little steps along the way. The practical strategies offered in this chapter will help you support your child as they embrace new experiences with confidence.

1. Focus on the effort, not the result

When a child feels like they're valued only when they win or succeed, they may start thinking that losing or failing makes them less important. Instead of praising your child only when they succeed, praise them for their effort. Giving your child positive feedback for trying teaches them that the effort is worthwhile, regardless of the outcome. They'll learn that trying sometimes leads to failure, and that's okay. But trying is also the only way to succeed, even if they have to fail a few times along the way.

When your child receives a good grade or result, celebrate their effort instead of the final product. Saying "I'm proud of how hard you worked" shows that trying matters, even if things don't go perfectly. If you focus only on results, your child may seek perfection, which can contribute to their fear of failing. Parents who set unrealistic expectations or react harshly to failures may inadvertently increase their child's anxiety and fear of disappointing their parents.

Younger children should be encouraged for their efforts as well. Let's consider this situation: A five-year-old wants to make their own bed in the morning. They'll likely try their best to make their bed look the same as when their parent makes it. But usually the result will fall short. Praising this child for their effort will encourage them to try again the next time.

It can help to share stories about failure with your child. They may be surprised and inspired to discover that some famously successful people have also had to face failure. Let's take Michael Jordan as an example. He was cut from his high school basketball team, but he kept on playing. He said, "I have missed more than 9,000 shots in my career. I have lost almost 300 games. On 26 occasions I have been entrusted to take the game-winning shot, and I missed. I have failed over and over and over again in my life. And that is why I succeed."

You can also consider Abraham Lincoln's list of failures, setbacks, and successes from the Library of Congress Online Catalog to explain how important it is to always try again:

- Lost job in 1832
- Defeated for state legislature in 1832
- Failed in business in 1833
- Elected to state legislature in 1834
- Sweetheart died in 1835
- Had nervous breakdown in 1836
- Defeated for Speaker in 1838
- Defeated for nomination for Congress in 1843
- Elected to Congress in 1846
- Lost renomination in 1848
- Rejected for land officer in 1849
- Defeated for U.S. Senate in 1854
- Defeated for nomination for Vice President in 1856
- Again defeated for U.S. Senate in 1858
- Elected President in 1860

You can reframe failure as a natural and valuable part of the learning process. We need only look at Michael Jordon and Abraham Lincoln to see how trying again can build character and lead to success.

2. Make home a safe place for making mistakes

Making mistakes in public can be humiliating and sometimes terrifying for children. Home can feel safer for a child, as they feel free from the scrutiny of their peers and teachers. When your child makes a mistake, instead of reprimanding them, talk it out with them so that you both understand why the mistake happened and perhaps how to avoid something similar in the future. This will help alleviate the fear of making mistakes.

Children don't make mistakes on purpose; mistakes are usually the result of an error in judgement. For example, if your child breaks a table lamp while running to the door to meet a friend, the error in judgement was running faster than they were able to navigate the turns needed to get to the door. In that moment, your child likely feels bad about the mistake, so reprimanding them will only make them feel worse. Talking to them about the cause of the mistake can help them avoid doing something similar in the future.

Remind your child that mistakes are a natural part of learning, and that everyone makes mistakes, including you. Share stories about times when you made mistakes and what you learned. This helps them to see mistakes as something everyone experiences and not as something to fear.

Making mistakes is an important part of your child's development. When children are allowed to make mistakes and learn from them, they grow into adults who are more confident and capable.

3. Encourage your child to explore new activities and hobbies

Activities, hobbies, and sports are a great way for children to develop skills and learn to deal with failure and setbacks. When your child decides to try something new, it's important to help them set realistic goals. If possible, they can set multiple small goals that will lead to attaining a larger goal. For example, if your child wants to audition for a starring role in the school play, but they've never acted before, you could suggest that they audition for a smaller role first. This may be a more attainable goal, which will help them feel less fearful of the audition process and more confident to try again another time.

For some children, breathing exercises or positive self-talk can help them prepare for something that they're hesitant to try. Having constructive conversations with your child about failure can mitigate emotional setbacks from failures. If they're not sure they'll be good at a new activity, you can remind them that trying something new can be fun and rewarding and that enjoying the new activity is more important than being good at it. For example, playing in a swimming pool can be fun, even if you aren't a good swimmer.

4. Model how to face fear of failure

Children learn a lot from watching their parents — and children are always watching their parents. When you face a situation in which you're afraid of failing, talk to your child about how you feel and why it's important to persevere. For example, if you've decided to look for a new job, you may be afraid that you won't get the job you've applied for, or you may find the interview process overwhelming and scary. If your child sees you practicing your interview skills, they'll learn that it's important to prepare for these situations. If you don't get the job, you can show your child that it's not the end of the world: There are other jobs you can apply for, and you now have some practice with interviews.

How you react to situations is important because children will often look to a parent to determine how they should react to a given experience. For example, a toddler may fall while running. If their parent reacts with a gasp and runs to check on them, the child may start to cry, as their parent's reaction has caused them to feel that the situation is scary and maybe dangerous. However, if their parent reacts calmly, the child is more likely to get up and move on without any fuss.

5. Offer your child help, but don't take over

This is one of the most important rules of good parenting. If your child is struggling, give them gentle support, but let them keep trying on their own. For example, if they're dressing themselves or setting the table and they get stuck, give them a small hint instead of doing it for them. This builds their confidence and shows that you believe in their abilities. If a child can do it by themselves, let them. It may take more time and patience, and the results might be messy, but it's usually good enough.

6. Celebrate the little steps along the way

If your child is working hard on something, recognize each small achievement. This helps them feel proud of their progress and encourages them to keep going. Sometimes a task or chore may look too big to attempt. However, if you divide the task into small steps and encourage your child to do one step at a time, it can give them courage to start the task. Once they have successfully completed the first step, they'll be more likely to continue.

With these simple strategies, you can help your child to feel more confident about trying new things without a fear of failing. Encouraging and allowing children to try things on their own takes patience and time, but in the end, you'll help your child face difficulties and failures with confidence and perseverance.

Reflection Questions

Have I ever been afraid of trying something new? How did I handle it?

Have I ever been tempted to take over when my child is struggling with a task?

CHAPTER 3

HELPING CHILDREN COPE

WITH SETBACKS

AND DISAPPOINTMENTS

Where there is no struggle, there is no strength.

— Oprah Winfrey

Throughout their life your child will inevitably face setbacks and disappointments. Whether it's failing a test, losing a game, or not getting invited to a party, these moments can feel overwhelming. Learning how to cope with these types of things when they're young helps children handle setbacks and disappointments when they're older and on their own or when you're not available to help them.

Learning how to navigate these challenges is essential for building resilience. Parents play an important role in guiding their children through disappointments and helping them develop the emotional tools to bounce back stronger. Parents can do this by acknowledging their children's feelings, modelling resilience, teaching problem-solving skills, encouraging positive thinking, providing comfort and support, avoiding overprotection, and encouraging persistence.

1. Acknowledge their feelings

When children experience a disappointment, it's important for parents to recognize and validate their emotions. Brushing off their feelings with statements like "It's not a big deal" or "You'll get over it" dismisses their real experience and feelings. Instead, take time to listen and acknowledge their distress. A statement like "I can see that you're really upset, and that's okay" shows them that their feelings matter and that it's natural to feel disappointed at times. This validation builds trust and opens the door for your child to talk to you about what's upsetting them. Ask your child what's bothering them, give them your full attention, and listen to what they say. They'll feel validated and comforted, and then you can help them sort out what to do next.

2. Model resilience

Your children are always watching you and learning from your behaviour. Children learn how to handle setbacks by watching how their parents handle difficulties or setbacks. If you demonstrate calmness, problem-solving, and a positive attitude when faced with difficulties, you're modelling resilient behaviour, and your children will likely mimic that. On the other hand, if your children see you dissolve into chaos when something goes wrong, they'll learn that helplessness and chaos are normal reactions to setbacks.

If something doesn't go your way, talk about it in a positive way and show how you keep trying. Your child can learn by seeing how you work your way through a problem. This doesn't mean you need to hide your emotions or your distress. After your initial reaction, you can demonstrate to your child how you figure out what to do and how to do it.

Consider this scenario: Suppose you've invited your in-laws for dinner, and you spent the day shopping and cooking special dishes that you know they'll like. You set your table, paying particular attention to details like fresh flowers, pretty serviettes, and candles. You showered, fixed your hair, and put on a fresh outfit. Just before they're expected to arrive, they call to say they forgot about the dinner and have other plans now. They offer to come next week instead. Understandably, you're disappointed and angry. You might want to abruptly end the call and yell at your husband about how inconsiderate his parents are.

But if we want to teach our kids how to handle stressful situations, it starts with staying calm and taking the time to think through the problem. You're still upset, but instead of taking it out on other people, you can demonstrate a healthier way to deal with disappointment. You might start by telling your in-laws that you'll call them back later, so you don't have to talk to them while you're emotional. Instead of yelling at your husband, you can let him know him how disappointed you are and that you need some space to think and to decide what to do next.

Sharing your experiences and explaining how you dealt with difficult situations teaches your child that upsets are normal, but they aren't usually devastating. This not only normalizes setbacks as part of life but also shows that recovery is possible. When parents model resilience, they provide a blueprint for their children to follow.

3. Teach problem-solving skills

When your child faces disappointment, it's important to validate their feelings and to help them figure out how to deal with it. Rather than rescuing your child from their disappointment, help them solve the problem. Encourage your child to think about what they could do differently next time or how they might handle a similar situation better.

Ask your child questions to help them reflect on their situation: "What do you think you could try next time?" or "What would help you feel better about this?" This shifts the focus from feeling helpless to taking action, empowering children to take control of future challenges.

4. Encourage positive thinking

One of the most powerful ways to help children deal with disappointment is by fostering the belief that their abilities and their thinking can be developed through effort. When your child fails, remind them that it's an opportunity to learn and improve rather than a reflection of their inherent worth. Asking them what they can learn from a failure or reminding them that mistakes help us grow reinforces the idea that setbacks are stepping stones toward growth, not dead ends.

5. Provide comfort and support

While it's important to help children develop coping skills, it's equally important to offer emotional support. Reassure your child that they are loved and valued no matter what. Let them know that one setback doesn't define who they are or their future success. This provides a sense of security and helps your child build the confidence to try again. A simple hug or a few kind words can usually go a long way in comforting a disappointed child.

6. Avoid overprotection

It's natural for parents to want to shield their children from disappointment, but overprotection can hinder their development. By constantly intervening or solving problems for them, parents rob their children of the opportunity to learn how to cope with failure, setbacks, and disappointment on their own. When parents solve every problem, children start to believe that they don't have the ability to solve their own problems.

Allowing your child to experience manageable disappointments — such as being cut from a team or losing a competition — is important for their development. It's in these moments of discomfort that your child can develop the problem-solving skills they need to handle setbacks and emerge stronger.

7. Encourage persistence

Lastly, teach your child the value of trying again. Help them understand that setbacks are not signals to give up but opportunities to keep trying. When children encounter failure and disappointment, encourage them to try again or approach the situation with a new strategy. Celebrate your child's efforts, regardless of the outcome, and remind them that persistence often leads to success in the long run.

As adults, we know that setbacks and disappointments are inevitable, so how your child learns to cope with them is critical for their emotional growth. By acknowledging your child's feelings, modelling resilience, teaching problem-solving skills, and fostering a positive mindset, you can give your child the tools to navigate challenges with confidence. It's through these experiences that your child develops the resilience needed to thrive in an unpredictable world.

Reflection Questions

How do I model resilience?

How do I teach problem-solving skills to my child?

CHAPTER 4

SAFE RISK-TAKING

*You'll never be bored when you try something
new. There's really no limit to what you can do.*

— Dr. Seuss

One of the more challenging tasks of parenthood is trying
to decide how much independence to give your child and
how much protection from hurts and disappointments
they need from you. The proportion of protection to
independence, of course, shifts as your child grows older.
A newborn needs us to do everything for them. A young
child still needs a lot of protection. A young adult, on the
other hand, can usually do everything for themselves and
so needs very little protection.

This shift from complete protection to independence
is gradual. Most children want to do things themselves at
a very early age. Their pushes for independence involve
taking risks: learning to walk, to go down the stairs, to feed

themselves. As a child grows older, they take greater risks when they learn to ride a bike, to swim, or to skate. Adolescents take even bigger risks when learning to drive a car, becoming involved in a romantic relationship, and making decisions about their future education. Taking risks is the only way a child can grow into an independent adult.

As a parent, your role is to teach your children to take safe or healthy risks. What is a healthy risk? According to Katie Hurley in her *HealthCentral* article "Resilience in Children: Strategies to Strengthen Your Kids," a healthy risk is "something that pushes a child to go outside of their comfort zone, but results in very little harm if they are unsuccessful."

So what do you need to protect your child from? And what should you encourage your child to do on their own? In the past, parents would protect their children from drowning in a local pond or running into a busy street or venturing so far away that they would become lost. They believed this was about as much protection as a child needed to be safe from harm. Parents were primarily concerned with protecting their children from physical harm in their immediate environment. They would never have considered riding a bicycle, participating in sports, playing unsupervised with friends, or skating on a local pond to be unusually risky behaviour.

Most parents today practice some safe risk-taking with their children. For example, they'll have their child wear a bicycle helmet and teach them to swim. However, we should also be encouraging our children to practice safe risk-taking for themselves. Most activities that children take part in today are supervised by an adult, so there's little opportunity for a child to take risks on their own.

What has changed to make today's parents feel the need to protect their child from risks such as getting hurt while riding a bicycle or playing sports? Why do parents feel they must protect their child from any hurts or disappointments? There are several factors in our modern society that have led to concerns about safety and aversion to risk.

Child-focused family life

Caregivers today focus more on the needs and welfare of their children than in the past, sometimes to the exhaustion of the parents. Families also tend to have fewer children, averaging only one or two, compared to the larger families from years past. Because families are smaller, parents have more time to spend with each child. But it's also common for both parents to work full-time. This often leads to feeling guilty about being away all day, and so parents tend to spend what free time they have with their children. Interestingly, research suggests that, contrary to popular belief, parents today spend more one-on-one time with their children than in the past, when it was more common for only one parent to work outside of the home.

Today's parents have also become highly attuned to their children's emotional well-being. Many have increasingly made their child's happiness and self-esteem a primary focus. Of course, happiness and strong self-esteem are to be desired, but they can't be imposed from the outside. These are things that a child fosters within themselves. They do this by experiencing successes and failures, which they have learned to deal with appropriately.

Social media

Social media has bombarded parents with infinite amounts of information on how to parent children — and specifically — how to keep their children safe and healthy. There's no end to information about child safety and emotional child welfare, as well as tips and hints on how to raise children who are perfectly healthy and happy.

Having access to all this information and advice burdens parents with the chore of trying to raise the perfect child. There's always the temptation to compare what you're doing with what other parents are doing or what parenting information suggests you should be doing. So it's not surprising that parents might feel overwhelmed with the responsibility of doing all they can do to make their children happy.

Regulation of most childhood activity

A large part of a young child's day may be spent in daycare or school. These institutions have become highly regulated to support the physical and emotional health of young students. Additionally, most children's activities outside of school, such as sports, camps, and extracurriculars, are also regulated. The downside of this regulation is that there's little room for unsupervised play and few opportunities for risk-taking.

Fear of emotional distress

Some parents today fear that their child will fail, wilt, or crumble emotionally if they are disappointed or hurt. Others believe that a child might become inhibited or crushed if their thoughts and behaviours are controlled or curbed in any way. It's understandable to want to protect your children from emotional pain. And research shows that children thrive when they are protected from inappropriate or unsafe behaviour. But within a reasonably safe environment, children should be encouraged to function independently, even if the result will cause them some emotional distress.

A more dangerous world

Many parents are concerned that the world has become more dangerous. They fear their child might be abducted while walking to school or playing outside or that they'll fall victim to internet predators. While today's world is more dangerous and these incidents do happen, they're not as common as parents fear.

Most child abductions are committed by someone the child knows, often a family member. In fact, 78% of abductors are the non-custodial parent (Child Find of America 2024).

Parents can help protect their children by teaching them the importance of street smarts. Children will eventually be alone within their community, and they need to know how to handle themselves when this happens. Teach your child to be cautious around unfamiliar adults, to trust their instincts, and to recognize when something feels wrong. Ensure they understand that they should never get into a car or walk off with a stranger. If they feel uneasy in a situation, they should know it's okay to leave immediately. Encourage your children to call home if they ever feel unsafe or need to be picked up, whether from a park, a party, or elsewhere. If they don't have a cellphone, teach them to seek the help of a trusted neighbour or adult or to go to a nearby store.

Parents should also teach their children about safe internet use. Most young children today have access to a phone or computer. Many of their school projects involve the use of a computer. We can't cut the computer from our children's lives as it is an intricate part of modern life. Explain to your child why they should never give out personal information or pictures of themselves to people online without your consent.

While these modern-day factors may affect the way you parent your children, it's still important to give them the opportunity to take safe risks based on their ages and abilities.

For younger children:

- Let them play alone in the backyard with or without friends — making up their own games or activities.

- Let them climb on stairs or play on furniture.

- Let them learn to ride a bike without training wheels.

- Let them try new foods.

- Let them play on playground equipment, climbing walls or ladders alone.

- Let them take part in sports activities.

When your older child seems to be ready:

- Let them go to a local store to buy a treat for themselves.

- Let them ride their bike to school.

- Let them walk to school with a group of neighbourhood children.

- Let them go to a local playground with friends.

Children who are allowed to take safe risks are more likely to develop a sense of self-competence and self-value. As children become used to facing challenges by themselves and overcoming their fears, their anxiety and fear of failure will decrease. So the balance is weighing the known risks that exist with your child's ability to handle those risks. Understandably, this also means that parents will feel some anxiety. However, each child must be allowed to test their own limits, which means that parents must balance protection with independence.

Reflection Questions

How can I encourage my child to be independent?

How can I give my child some safe unsupervised time?

CHAPTER 5

TAKING RESPONSIBILITY FOR

DECISIONS AND BEHAVIOUR

You grow through what you go through.

— Tyrese Gibson

Perhaps one of the most important behaviours that contribute to a child's resilience is taking responsibility for the decisions they make and the things they do. To learn how to take responsibility, a child must experience the natural consequences of their decisions and their behaviours. For example, if your child forgets to take their homework to school, it's not helpful for you to rush in and deliver it. Let them experience the consequences that their teacher sets out for not turning in homework. Your child will learn that remembering to take their homework to school is their responsibility — not yours.

A child learns accountability when they're the one who makes the decision. For example, if your child refuses to wear a heavy coat on a cold day, you may point out that it's very cold outside and explain the consequences of not wearing the coat. If they still refuse to wear a heavy coat, let them wear their lightweight jacket. If they're cold that day, they'll likely make a better decision next time.

Part of helping your child become responsible for themselves is to teach them to make good choices, consider consequences, cope with difficult situations, and reflect on past decisions.

Making good choices

Help your child make informed decisions and make sure they have all the information they need to evaluate the pros and cons of their decisions. If your child is trying to decide whether to take ballet or figure skating lessons this winter, talk to them about the things they should consider, such as the time commitment, cost, benefits to them, and their happiness — that is, which activity would bring them more joy. Once you've talked it over, let them make the decision. Ensure they understand ahead of time that they should commit to their decision once it's made. Carrying through with ballet or figure skating lessons is just as important as the decision itself. They learn that they can't quit something they've committed to until it's complete. This teaches them, integrity, grit, and resilience.

Even very young children must start making decisions for themselves. The decisions may be small, like whether to have a scoop of vanilla or chocolate ice cream. But they learn that they must choose — they can't have both. You might suggest to your child that they have vanilla this time and chocolate next time. This type of problem-solving also helps them to learn to wait for some of the things they want until another time.

Considering consequences

Help your child consider the possible consequences of their decision by giving them questions they can ask themselves. Here are some examples:

- What might happen if I choose option A? What if I choose option B?
- Who will this affect besides me?
- If I make the wrong decision, will I be okay with it?
- Is there a plan C?

Once your child has made the decision, encourage them to follow through with it. Many parents struggle with this approach because they feel their child didn't make the best decision. But it's important not to threaten that they'll regret their decisions by saying things like "Don't blame me if it doesn't work" or "Don't expect me to bail you out if you get into trouble." You can be almost sure that if your child fails in what they decided to do, they'll be reluctant to let you know. Support their decisions even if you don't agree with them by saying something like "I'm not sure that's the best decision. But if it doesn't work out, let me know and we'll see what we can do to make it better."

Coping with struggles

Allow your child to struggle when it's appropriate. As parents, we should not solve all of our children's problems for them. If your child has a school project that they have to do at home, you can ensure they have all the materials needed for the project, but then you should allow them to complete the project by themselves. If they struggle, encourage them but don't do it for them. If they leave it to the last minute, let them hand in a rushed or incomplete project and receive an inferior mark. They'll likely complete the next project on time.

If your child continues to struggle with school assignments — doing them at the last minute or putting little effort into them — it's time to talk to them about why they're doing this. Maybe they find it too difficult or boring, or maybe they'd rather play video games. Only after you find out why your child is struggling can you help them find a solution.

Reflecting on past decisions

Help your child reflect on past decisions. Whether it was a good or a bad decision, talking about why it did or didn't go well will help them think through future decisions. Ask if they would make any changes the next time they have to make the same decision. If the decision they made was a bad one, help them think it through rather than punishing them for it.

The long-term benefit of helping a child learn how to make good decisions when they're young is that it will help them to make better decisions as an adult. Allowing your child to make their own decisions can make you feel anxious. However, you must learn to trust them if they're ever going to learn to trust themselves. They'll become more responsible, independent, and resilient as an adult.

Reflection Questions

Can I trust my child to make good decisions?

What do I do when my child makes a decision that I think is wrong?

CONCLUSION

Character cannot be developed in ease and quiet. Only through experience of trial and suffering can the soul be strengthened, vision cleared, ambition inspired, and success achieved.

— Helen Keller

As parents, our instinct is to shield our children from pain, failure, and hardship. We try to smooth the rough edges of their lives in an effort to keep them safe and happy. However, as we've explored throughout this book, too much protection doesn't create strength; it fosters fragility. It's with scraped knees, difficult conversations, and moments of doubt that children learn to navigate the complexities of life. We must have the courage to step back and allow our children to step forward.

No matter what approach you take to child rearing, whether it's authoritative, free-range, or gentle, you can incorporate a culture of "freedom with responsibility" for your child. If you allow your child to take risks and make decisions for themselves and to take responsibility for their behaviour and live with the consequences if they make a mistake, then you're preparing them to leave the shelter of your home and join the ranks of young adults without feeling overwhelmed, anxious, or depressed.

This is the ultimate learning experience for a young child, no matter their physical or mental abilities — resilience can be fostered in all children. And resilience and independence are the foundations of a successful life. As a final note, here are ten key questions you can ask yourself:

1. Before I intervene, is this something my child could do by themselves?
2. Am I allowing my child to take responsibility for their own decisions?
3. Am I over-planning my child's activities?
4. Am I giving my child enough time to be bored?
5. Am I allowing my child some unsupervised time, alone or with their friends?
6. Am I encouraging my child to take risks?
7. Do I allow my child to fail?
8. Do I model resilience?
9. Am I teaching my child problem-solving skills?
10. Am I promoting independence?

Teaching children to not fear failure, to take safe risks, to cope with setbacks and disappointments, and to take responsibility for their decisions will help prepare them for their adult lives. And when they're ready to fly the nest, knowing that they are resilient enough to face the world will give you peace of mind.

As Heather Shumaker, author of *It's OK to Go Up the Slide*, says: "Instead of limiting healthy risk of all types, we need to limit structured time and grant kids more independence. Train your children. Set smart limits. Let them practice. Then let them go."

APPENDIX I:

PRACTICAL TIPS FOR PARENTS

The parents and professionals I interviewed for this book gave me practical suggestions that helped them instill resilience in their children, and they may help you too. In addition, I've gleaned some tips from other authors who've written about bringing up resilient, independent children. All these tips will not necessarily apply to you and your unique relationship with your child, but you may find some of them helpful in this wonderful journey of preparing your child for their future.

Encourage children to do things on their own

- As soon as your child is two or three years old, teach them how to put their toys away when they're finished with them. You might say, "Can you put away the biggest toy and I'll put away the smallest toy." Or, when they're a little older and know their colours, you might say, "Can you put away all the red toys and I'll put away all the blue toys," and so on. This teaches children at a very early age to pick up after themselves. They're learning how to be responsible.

- By the time your child is four years old, teach them how to make their bed in the morning. They're not going to make the bed perfectly, but they'll make an attempt at it and that's what matters. They'll gradually get better at it as they get older but the expectation is that they'll always make their bed when they get up in the morning. Again they're learning to take responsibility for themselves.

- Teach your child to make their own school lunch. Make sure you have the food on hand that they like, but let *them* take the responsibility of actually making their own lunch.

- Give your child age-appropriate chores to do around the house. These might be simple things, like feeding their pet every day, setting the table, or hanging up their coat when they come in from outside. When these chores are agreed upon by you and your child, it's important to follow up and make sure that they've kept up their commitment. This helps the child to begin to understand the meaning of integrity or following through when they've agreed to do something.

- If your child is given a school project to be completed at home, give them some help if they ask but don't do it for them. It's better for your child to receive a medium grade that they earned themselves than an A that you earned for them. It also gives them an opportunity to learn where they may be able to improve or where they made a mistake.

Allowance and "giving back"

- When your child is old enough to understand money, you can start giving them an allowance. It's important to go over what the allowance is for. You can discuss the various options, such as spending it freely, spending some and saving some, or saving it all. This exercise teaches your child that when their allowance is spent, there's no more money until they receive the next allowance. This helps a child develop a sense of how much things cost and teaches them to save for something in the future. Families I interviewed gave me some thoughts and examples of how they manage allowances:

  o Parents provide their children with the necessary equipment or tools for any sport or activity that they're involved in, and their child saves their own money for extra things that they may not need but that they want.

  o Children may have their own money from saving their allowance or from birthday gifts. Saving helps a child to be future-oriented, to develop patience, and to be prudent when spending their money.

- o One family started a "nut jar" for their young family. Whenever one of their children did something extra or showed some patience or kindness to others in the family, they got one or two nuts put into their jar. If they misbehaved (for example, if they hit their sibling) they lost a nut. Nuts could then be used for extra treats, such as staying up a little later to watch TV.

- Teach your child to be charitable and kind to other children. This may involve encouraging your child to share some of what they have with another child who has less and helping your child to become more compassionate and empathetic toward children who have disabilities. It also teaches them to be more understanding of the behaviour of some of their friends. Volunteering and helping others is important for creating self-worth and resilience in a young person. They learn they have something of worth to offer others.

Encourage effort

- Always praise your child for effort. Encourage them to do their best and reassure them that if they do, the outcome is always acceptable. Your child will learn to feel good about themselves if you recognize that they've tried as hard as they can.

Control emotions

- Teach your child to express their emotions openly when appropriate and to contain them when the time is not appropriate. For example, most parents would agree that a child screaming at a supermarket check-out because they can't have a candy is not an acceptable expression of their emotion. Ignoring this behaviour, as difficult as that may be, while at the same time repeating to your child that they can't have what they're crying for is the right response to this behaviour. If you give into the child and buy them a candy to stop them from crying, they've learned that they can get what they want by crying. On the other hand, crying when they come home from school because they haven't been invited to a classmate's birthday party is appropriate. This is a time when a child needs to be consoled and helped to understand why that may have happened and how to handle it.

- Help your child think through failures. Failures and disappointments are part of life, and helping your child deal with something that has hurt or disappointed them is an important factor in developing resilience. For example, some parents might suggest to a child who has failed a test that they try again but study or practice harder, emphasizing that failure is not an end and does not define them but that it's an opportunity to learn and grow.

The outside world

- "Physical play, outdoors and with children of mixed ages, is the healthiest most natural, most beneficial sort of play. Play with some degree of physical risk is essential because it teaches children how to look after themselves and each other" (Haidt, 2024).

- "It is in unsupervised *child-led* play that children best learn to tolerate bruises, handle their emotions, read other children's emotions, take turns, resolve conflicts, and play fair. Children are intrinsically motivated to acquire these skills because they want to be included in the playgroup and they want to keep the fun going" (Haidt, 2024).

- Do not expect your child's teacher to fix everything that's wrong in your child's life. The teacher's job is to teach — your job is to parent. Remember that most teachers have around thirty students in their class and they can't be expected to give a lot of individual attention to each one every day. Of course, a good teacher will try to nurture each student and bring out the best in each of them. But if a child is experiencing severe emotional problems, the teacher alone can't be expected to be the main source of therapy for the child. This is when parents and professionals outside of the school system all need to collaborate with the teacher to contribute to that child's growth.

- Having a stable, caring adult in a child's life is foundational to building resilience. This may be a parent, a grandparent, a teacher, a coach, or a neighbour. This adult can provide a secure base from which the child can explore the world, knowing they have someone they can rely on in times of difficulty or uncertainty. This relationship fosters a sense of trust, which is essential for the child to feel safe enough to take risks, make mistakes, and learn from them, ultimately strengthening their resilience.

- Participation in sports and team activities is an excellent experience for children. It can teach them how to cooperate with teammates, take direction from a coach or a captain, cope with failure and disappointment when they lose, and celebrate when they win. If your child doesn't enjoy sports, they can participate in other group activities, such as a school play, a choir, or summer camp, which can offer them the same benefits. However, participation in group activities may not appeal to all children. Some children prefer more solitary activities, such as reading, drawing, or playing alone. If the child is happy doing solitary activities, leave them be. Not all children are outgoing or seek constant interaction with other children. Extroversion or outgoingness are often highly prized, and being able to socialize with other children is desirable, but it's important not to force a child who is inclined to be introverted to always join in with others.

- Watch the news together and talk about it with your children. It's not possible to protect your children from what's happening in the world around them. They see the news on TV, they hear stories from their friends, and they hear Mom and Dad discussing events. Some of these things, such as news of wars, famine, pandemics, severe weather, fires, school shootings, or child abductions, may scare your child. It's important to discuss these things with your child realistically but with an emphasis on whether or not any of these are likely to happen to them. Remind them of the protections that are in place in their community and the protections that you as a parent will provide.

Screen time

- Some people advocate that children should not have smartphones before high school and should not have social media before the age of sixteen.

- Advocates for phone-free schools claim it's the only way to free up children's attention for each other and for their teachers.

- Some parents believe that children should not have phones in their bedroom after eight at night. Many don't allow them to have their phones at the dinner table when they're eating together. Others prohibit screens while out for a walk, when in restaurants, when company is over, on play dates or other social occasions, or even when in the car together.

- Parents need to model appropriate screen time themselves.

- We don't need to reject technology. We need to put it in its place.

- Many children are overstimulated by social media and computer games. Children need some mental downtime in order to daydream, fantasize, plan, and reflect.

Your personal relationship with your child

- Children do not respond well to loud voices or being yelled at.

- Assure your child that they can talk to you about anything no matter what it is.

- Give your child some free time away from you, whether it's biking around the block, playing with other children on the street, or going to the store to buy a treat by themselves.

- Let your child know that there are limits on their behaviour. For example, running wild through someone else's house is probably not allowed, but running wild at a playground may be just fine.

- Let your child know that you also have limits. Don't let them push you to the point of exhaustion.

- It's okay to say no to your child. Sometimes you have to say it with little or no explanation, such as when there's some urgency and it's necessary to stop your child's behaviour. For example, if you're crossing a busy road and your child wants to stop in the middle to pick up a pretty leaf, saying no is required for safety. You can explain your reasoning later. Sometimes your child has heard your reasons for not giving your permission to do something, and they continue to disagree with you. A simple no can be the end of the discussion.

- One of my supervisors in childcare once said to me about a parent's relationship to their child: "Remember, you are bigger than he is, you are smarter than he is, and you are wiser than he is."

Street smarts

- "Kids need to know what to do when they're lost — if a child is in trouble, she needs to be able to identify the helpers. These are usually strangers. And in many communities helpful strangers include police officers, firefighters, medics and other officials along with store clerks. More often it is another parent or a friendly face in the crowd who understands kids. Some parents recommend their child find a mom or a dad who has children with them" (Shumaker, 2016).

- Children can learn how to get a book out of the library by themselves, take the bus to school, walk to a nearby store, and cross a busy street safely.

These are only a few of the many suggestions that I

heard from parents and professionals. You will be able to decide when your own child is ready to try riskier activities and at what age to try them.

APPENDIX II:

LIST OF CHILDREN'S BOOKS ABOUT RESILIENCE

Overcoming Challenges and Problem-Solving

The Rabbit Listened (Cori Doerrfeld) — A gentle story about how sometimes the best way to help someone struggling is simply to listen.

The Most Magnificent Thing (Ashley Spires) — A young girl learns perseverance as she works through frustration to build something incredible.

Even Superheroes Have Bad Days (Shelly Becker) — Superheroes feel emotions too, but they use resilience to make good choices.

A Perfectly Messed-Up Story (Patrick McDonnell) — A fun take on handling imperfection and learning to go with the flow.

The Girl Who Never Made Mistakes (Mark Pett & Gary Rubinstein) — A perfectionist learns the joy of making mistakes and embracing failure.

After the Fall (How Humpty Dumpty Got Back Up) (Dan Santat) — A story about Humpty Dumpty overcoming fear and failure to rise again.

The Recess Queen (Alexis O'Neill) — A lesson in handling bullies and standing up for oneself.

The Sandwich Swap (Queen Rania Al Abdullah & Kelly DiPucchio) — Two friends navigate misunderstandings and differences in a lesson about acceptance.

I Can Do Hard Things: Mindful Affirmations For Kids (Gabi Garcia) — A mindfulness book encouraging self-belief and resilience.

Growth Mindset and Creativity

The Dot (Creatrilogy) (Peter H. Reynolds) — A young girl discovers the power of creativity and self-expression.

Ish (Creatrilogy) (Peter H. Reynolds) — Emphasizes that perfection isn't necessary — creativity is about trying.

Rosie Revere, Engineer (Andrea Beaty) — A young inventor learns to embrace failure as part of innovation.

Ada Twist, Scientist (Andrea Beaty) — A curious girl's scientific inquiries teach the value of persistence.

Violet the Pilot (Steve Breen) — A young girl's love for invention leads to an inspiring aviation adventure.

Bike On, Bear! (Cynthea Liu) — A bear determined to ride a bike learns resilience through practice.

Zog (Julia Donaldson) — A dragon learns that persistence and teamwork help him reach his goals.

Emotional Regulation and Mindfulness

My Magic Breathh: Finding Calm Through Mindful Breathing (Nick Ortner & Alison Taylor) — Teaches children how breathing can help them manage emotions.

Ravi's Roar (Tom Percival) — A boy learns to handle anger and express emotions in a healthy way.

The Buddha at Bedtime Treasury (Dharmachari Nagaraja) — A collection of wisdom-filled stories teaching love, kindness, and inner strength.

Sad, The Dog (Sandy Fussell) — A heartwarming story about self-worth and finding a place to belong.

Courage and Standing Up for Yourself

Malala's Magic Pencil (Malala Yousafzai) — The true story of Malala's childhood dreams and her fight for education.

She Persisted: 13 American Women Who Changed the World (Chelsea Clinton) — Stories of real-life women who displayed extraordinary perseverance.

Strictly No Elephants (Lisa Mantchev) — A story about friendship, inclusion, and standing up for what's right.

Nothing Stopped Sophie: The Story of Unshakable Mathematician Sophie Germain (Cheryl Bardoe) — A true story about a mathematician's determination to solve an impossible equation.

Your Name Is a Song (Jamilah Thompkins-Bigelow) — A child learns to embrace the beauty of her unique name.

The Proudest Blue: A Story of Hijab and Family (Ibtihaj Muhammad) — A girl finds strength and pride in wearing her hijab despite bullying.

Kindness, Generosity, and Friendship

The Giving Tree (Shel Silverstein) — A classic story about unconditional giving and selflessness.

The Curious Garden (Peter Brown) — A boy's love for nature transforms a grey city into a thriving green space.

A Chair for My Mother (Vera B. Williams) — A girl helps her family save up for something special after a fire.

The Year We Learned to Fly (Jacqueline Woodson) — Encourages children to use their imagination to overcome life's difficulties.

Meesha Makes Friends (Tom Percival) — A child struggling to fit in learns how to make friends in her own way.

Perseverance and Hard Work

Emmanuel's Dream: The True Story of Emmanuel Ofosu Yeboah (Laurie Ann Thompson) — The true story of a boy with a disability who proves that nothing can hold him back.

The Little Engine That Could (Watty Piper) — A timeless tale about determination and believing in oneself.

Otis (Loren Long) — A tractor shows the importance of perseverance and kindness in helping a friend.

Jules Versus the Ocean (Jessie Sima) — A girl keeps trying to build the perfect sandcastle despite the ocean washing it away.

Whistle for Willie (Ezra Jack Keats) — A young boy is determined to learn how to whistle, despite many failed attempts.

APPENDIX III:

SOURCES AND FURTHER READING

FOR PARENTS

1. *The Anxious Generation: How the Great Rewiring of Childhood Is Causing an Epidemic of Mental Illness*

Jonathan Haidt, Penguin, 2024

A comprehensive book on the impact of social media on children and youth.

2. *Building Resilience in Children and Teens: Giving Kids Roots and Wings*

Kenneth R. Ginsburg and Martha M. Jablow, American Academy of Pediatrics, 2020

A comprehensive guide giving strategies to help children develop resilience, emphasizing the importance of balancing protection with independence.

3.   "How to Build Resilience in Children"

Australian Christian College Blog, October 27, 2017

This blog post provides practical tips for parents and educators to foster resilience in children, highlighting the role of supportive frameworks.

4.   "How to Incorporate Gentle Parenting in Your Everyday Life"

Lauren Mills, Parenting Mindfully Blog, retrieved from Australian Christian College Blog, February 16, 2024.

This guide offers insights into implementing gentle parenting techniques, focusing on empathy and positive reinforcement to build emotional resilience.

5.   "How to Quit Intensive Parenting"

Elliot Haspel, *The Atlantic*, May 10, 2022

Haspel discusses the drawbacks of intensive parenting and advocates for a more relaxed approach that allows children to develop autonomy and resilience.

6.   "Intensive Parenting Is Now the Norm in America"

Joe Pinsker, *The Atlantic*, January 16, 2019

Pinsker explores the cultural shift toward intensive parenting in the U.S. and its implications for both parents and children.

7.   *It's OK to Go Up the Slide: Renegade Rules for Raising Confident and Creative Children*

Heather Shumaker, Penguin Random House, 2016

Shumaker encourages parents to break conventional rules, promoting risk taking and independence to nurture creativity and confidence in children.

8.   "Lighthouse Parents Have More Confident Kids"

Russell Shaw, *The Atlantic*, September 22, 2024

Shaw introduces "Lighthouse Parenting," a balanced approach that combines guidance with allowing children to face challenges independently.

9.   "Parental Resilience: Protective and Promotive Factors"

Center for the Study of Social Policy, 2018

This guide outlines strategies for parents to build their own resilience, which in turn supports their children's emotional development.

10.   "Parenting Has Always Been Hard"

Jessica Grose, *New York Times*, September 11, 2024

Gross reflects on the timeless challenges of parenting and how modern societal changes have intensified pressures on parents.

11.   "Modern Parenting Is So Stressful That the U.S. Issued a Health Advisory. Parents Say It's Overdue"

Natalie Stechyson, *CBC News*, August 30, 2024

This article discusses the escalating stress levels among parents, leading to a national health advisory, and examines the impact on family resilience.

12.   "Parents Should Ignore Their Children More Often"

Darby Saxbe, *New York Times*, September 15, 2024

Saxbe suggests that over-involvement can hinder children's development, advocating for a hands-off approach to promote independence and resilience.

13.   "Raising Resilient Children and Youth"

Centre for Addiction and Mental Health (CAMH)

This resource offers evidence-based strategies focused on mental health to help parents and educators foster resilience in young people.

14.   "Resilience Guide for Parents and Teachers"

American Psychological Association, 2012

The APA provides practical advice emphasizing positive relationships and adaptive skills to help children manage stress and adversity.

15.   "Resilience in Children: Strategies to Strengthen Your Kids"

HealthCentral, November 24, 2020

This article offers expert advice on teaching problem-solving, encouraging independence, and managing emotions to build resilience in children.

16.   The Gift of Failure: How the Best Parents Learn to Let Go So Their Children Can Succeed

Jessica Lahey, Harper Collins, 2016

Lahey argues that allowing children to fail provides valuable learning experiences, fostering resilience and independence.

17.   "This Influencer Says You Can't Parent Too Gently"

Olga Khazan, *The Atlantic*, October 22, 2024

Khazan explores the gentle parenting movement, discussing its benefits and potential drawbacks in fostering resilience.

18.   "What Makes a Society More Resilient? Frequent Hardship"

Carl Zimmer, *New York Times*, May 1, 2024

Zimmer examines how societies that regularly face hardships tend to develop greater resilience, offering insights applicable to parenting.

19.   "Why Don't We Teach People How to Parent?"

Faith Hill, *The Atlantic*, February 2, 2024

Hill discusses the lack of formal education in parenting skills and the potential benefits of teaching effective parenting strategies to build resilient families.